How to Fail with Flying Colors

Your Guide to Ultimate Success

ISBN-13: 979-8-9928978-1-4

Cover design by: Vicky Wu, Unscrewed Publishing
Printed in the United States of America

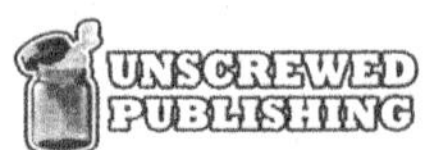

Author's Note

This book is a conversation between us—women balancing ambition, family, and the myth of "having it all." You'll see research and real-life experiences side by side because both matter. As you read, pause with me. Write in the margins, answer the prompts, and rediscover your own power. We're not fixing ourselves—we're reclaiming the truth that we were never broken.

Table of Contents

Introduction 7

Chapter 1: The Success Trap 9

Chapter 2: Redefining Failure 21

Chapter 3: Who Am I Without the Hustle 39

Chapter 4: The Weight of Guilt 53

Chapter 5: Redefining Success 67

Chapter 6: Sustaining Alignment 81

Chapter 7: Becoming the Success You Defined 91

Chapter 8: Celebrating the Wins 103

Chapter 9: Failing With Flying Colors: Your Turn 115

Conclusion — You Are the Success Story 125

Introduction

When I sat down to write this book I had no idea what I was doing. I fully expected to fail. I was pleasantly surprised to fail with flying colors and get this out into the world. It needed a push - and you will hear about it as we go along. I sat with this idea for years. I said "I will write it when…." What was I waiting for? I was waiting for a level of success that was externally measured to feel worthy to write my own story. Never again.

It is so easy to categorize all of the ways in which we fail - as mothers, as partners, in business, in our lives…in any and every capacity. I didn't realize how hardwired I was to fail until I started questioning why other people saw me in a way my mirror didn't reflect.

It's hard work failing with flying colors. I couldn't have done it without the people in my life who showed me what I couldn't see.

Thank you for picking up this book. My biggest wish is that I can help you change your reflection so it shows you the successful woman I know you are.

Grab your journal, let's get to work.

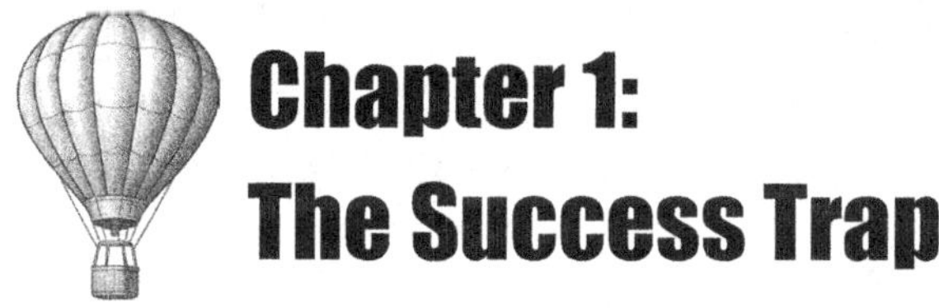

Chapter 1: The Success Trap

When Doing It All Still Feels Like Failure

I am the mom who sometimes gets to the carpool line early just to take a nap — because it's the only time in the day no one needs anything from me.

I am the mom who sometimes arrives at pickup later than planned because a client call ran over.

I am the woman who constantly feels like she's catching up, reacting, and trying not to drop anything.

The calendar says I should be in control.

The color-coded blocks tell a story of organization, calm, and mastery.

But one sick kid… a surprise school event… or my husband's forgotten deadline…

and the whole thing collapses like a tower of sticky notes.

I constantly question – what breaks first? The coffee pot or my sanity?

And the laundry?

Mostly clean. Definitely wrinkled.

Constantly living in baskets waiting for someone to go on a treasure hunt for socks.

We're told:

"Success should feel peaceful."

But most women I know are powered by caffeine, adrenaline, and that relentless whisper:

Why can't I keep up?

Power Pause

Take a deep breath. Where do you most feel the tension between "doing it all" and feeling fulfilled? Write it down before you keep reading.

The New Standard: Polished, Productive, Perfect

Scroll any feed and you'll meet the modern miracle worker—entrepreneur, mother, chef, volunteer, fitness coach, and self-care expert rolled into one. She's calm, styled, thriving…and completely exhausting to measure against.

Studies show that these polished snapshots aren't harmless. A University of Nebraska–Lincoln study found that new mothers who viewed idealized "mom-influencer" posts reported lower confidence and higher stress than mothers shown real-life images. And a 2021 meta-analysis confirmed that social media amplifies harmful self-comparison — especially among women juggling work and motherhood.

Our mothers compared themselves to the lady next door.

We compare ourselves to millions.

And I'll be honest — for a long time, those women made me feel inadequate.

> *Do they have a nanny we don't see?*
>
> *Do they even sweat?*
>
> *How do they keep their kids clean?*
>
> *Not long after?*

The sadness turned into irritation.

Why do THEY get to look rested? Why do THEY get to make this look easy?

The truth is, even the women who look perfect online struggle too—they just don't show it publicly. Society has taught us we must be everything: house manager, community volunteer, business owner, nurturer, and role model.

We are chasing curated illusions and wondering why our real life doesn't measure up.

I'm still learning that I can't measure myself against their projection—and that there's freedom in knowing I don't have to.

Power Pause

Open your journal and list three ways social media shapes what you think "success" should look like. Circle the one that feels heaviest to carry.

The Inherited Rulebook

Long before hashtags, women were handed a silent script called intensive mothering—the belief that good mothers are endlessly giving and self-sacrificing. Research consistently links this ideal to higher stress and lower life satisfaction.

Good mothers sacrifice.

Good mothers never complain.

Good mothers do everything.

Research calls this intensive mothering.

And women who believe it most strongly?

They experience more stress, guilt, and lower life satisfaction.

Even when we build businesses for flexibility, the old expectations follow. We become the CEO who still bakes the cupcakes, answers midnight emails, and feels guilty for wanting rest.

And this isn't new pressure—it's inherited. Generational studies show that perfectionism and stress echo through families. Many of us learned our standards from mothers who held everything together through scarcity or silence.

It's not just social media that teaches us our truths – look back on the wholesome family shows from the past – a man was the primary income earner and the woman did everything else, even if she worked outside of the home. Textbooks in school perpetuated these ideas as well – teaching young girls to grow into silent subservient wives. There is a whole era dedicated to the *Cult of Domesticity*.

The Cult of Domesticity was a prevailing ideology in the 19th century (especially in the U.S. and Britain) for upper- and middle-class women, defining acceptable femininity and the "proper sphere" of women. According to historian Barbara Welter (in her influential 1966 article "The Cult of True Womanhood: 1820-1860"), the "four cardinal virtues" of a "True Woman" were: piety, purity, submissiveness, and domesticity.

The ideology asserted that women belonged in the "private sphere" (home, family, moral center) while men belonged in the "public sphere" (work, politics, commerce). Educational materials, magazines (e.g., Godey's Lady's Book), advice books, and religious literature reinforced these standards.

Think about your childhood – it's filled with sacrifices your mother made that you didn't recognize at the time.

I never thought about what it meant for my Mom to pick me up from school instead of me taking the bus home. Never once considered what those days at home with me when I was sick cost her. Let's be clear – she always paid that cost.

My father didn't handle sick days, he didn't handle most of the driving me around. In fact – one time Mom had him pick me up from Girl Scouts and he showed back up at home without me. Why? He sat outside the meeting location, on an unlit street, in a black car with his lights off. I never knew he was there. My Mom came to get me.

As a mother we often carry the burden of doing it all and having to look good doing it. Thank goodness it's acceptable to wear yoga pants and a messy bun pretty much everywhere now!

My father worked hard, but he didn't work hard at carrying his share of the sacrifices a working parent makes. My first call growing up was always to my Mom. We are taught not to interrupt our fathers, their work is too important, they are too busy, and that their role is bread winner, not chef, not chauffeur, nor maid.

We didn't invent these rules; we inherited them. If you've been playing by that rulebook, you've been measuring success by someone else's definition. But now you get to write your own rules.

Power Pause

Think about a lesson you absorbed from your mother or grandmother about what a "good woman" does. Does that belief still serve you?

More Pressure, Fewer Boundaries

Modern working moms are stretched thinner than ever. Surveys show that two-thirds of working mothers now report anxiety or depression symptoms, and nearly seven in ten say they feel burned out. In small-business circles, researchers describe role overload—too many responsibilities, too few resources—as a direct predictor of stress and exhaustion.

Psychologists also identify the mental load: the invisible labor of remembering, planning, and coordinating everyone's lives. The mental load itself—not just physical work—drives much of our overwhelm.

We are living proof that we can be in multiple roles… but only in one body.

I've had days where all my roles collided:

Daughter caring for my father.

Mother attending school events.

Business owner serving clients.

Wife trying to stay connected.

Woman trying not to disappear inside all the labels.

There were nights lying awake counting dropped tasks instead of sheep….the calls not made, unanswered emails and the laundry sitting wrinkled in baskets. The guilt of not getting it all done ate away at me.

People tell me, "But you always seem to have it together" and I smile. My social media game face must be on point!

They don't see the caffeine, the missed calls, or the nights I stare at the ceiling calculating hours I can't get back. The fix wasn't instant—it came from learning to prioritize, define my own standards, and decide what I'm actually willing to carry.

Power Pause

List every role you currently hold. Which two drain you most when combined? What boundary could lighten that weight this week?

The Amplifier: Social Media Meets Generational Expectation

Our mothers carried guilt quietly; we carry it with notifications. Every scroll reignites an old standard—patience, perfection, productivity—filtered through someone else's highlight reel.

Recent cross-generational research shows younger mothers share their elders' values of care and sacrifice but now add technology management and "personal branding" to the list.

We inherited the same ideals...and added Wi-Fi.

> *No wonder we feel more overwhelmed than any women before us.*
>
> *No wonder success feels like a moving target.*
>
> *No wonder it feels like everyone else is ahead.*
>
> *None of us chose this — but all of us are navigating it.*

That's why today's women feel the pressure more acutely: ancestral expectations amplified by algorithms.

Power Pause

Notice how often your phone triggers self-criticism in a day. Could you silence one type of notification or unfollow one account that fuels comparison?

Reframing the Trap

If our definitions of success were written by women who survived on self-denial—and re-marketed by social-media highlight reels—then "failure" isn't proof we're broken. It's a signal that the ruler we're using is outdated.

When you catch yourself thinking I'm failing, pause and ask: *Whose measure am I using—and do I even believe in it?*

Here's the truth we never learned: You are not broken - your measuring stick is. Ask yourself:

- *Who told me I had to be everything?*
- *Who benefits when I exhaust myself?*
- *Why do I call it failure when it's actually humanity?*

The moment you ask those questions, the trap begins to lose its grip.

Power Pause

Which expectations in your life feel heavy? Circle the ones that are not truly yours.

- *Perfect house*
- *Perfect mothering*
- *Perfect business*
- *Being liked by everyone*
- *Doing it all without help*
- *Having it all — without rest*

Write one expectation you're ready to retire.

Final Power Practice – Reclaiming Your Measure

Take fifteen minutes to write your own definition of success—one that honors both ambition and rest.

1. *Identify three values that truly matter to you.*
2. *Describe how success looks when those values lead.*
3. *Choose one small action you'll take this week that aligns with that definition.*

You're not behind—you're breaking free of borrowed expectations. What once felt like failure is proof you're evolving. Let's carry that truth forward into Chapter 2, where we'll explore how "failing with flying colors" becomes the foundation for lasting success.

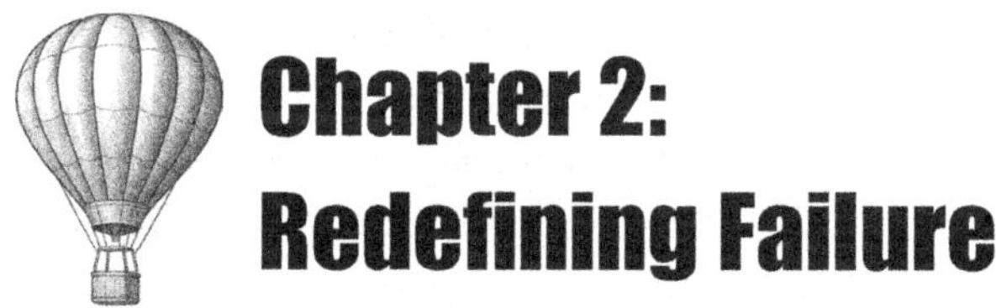

Chapter 2: Redefining Failure

The Expectation of Failure

When I think about failure, one thing that has stuck with me for years is that the expectation of it was taught to me long before I ever experienced it.

When I was in high school, I'd stay up late writing English papers, pouring my energy into getting every sentence right. Before I turned them in, my dad would proofread them. Without fail, he'd hand them back and say, "It's a C paper at best," or "You're not going to do well on this."

And more often than not, I'd come home with an A. I'd show him -feeling proud and ready to prove him wrong - only to hear "That's because your teachers are stupid and they don't know what they are talking about."

Here's what I understand now: I didn't fail those papers. I met the standard set by the people who were evaluating me. But it felt like failure, because the person who was supposed to be leading and guiding me couldn't recognize my success. His approval was a moving target—and to this day, I've never quite identified where that bar actually is.

That experience planted something deep in me: the belief that no matter how well I perform, it's never enough. And if it's never enough, then it must be failure.

Years later, that same dynamic showed up again. When my husband and I got custody of his 14-year-old daughter, we weren't thriving financially. We brought her home, got her what she needed, applied for and received Medicaid and food stamps. It wasn't glamorous—but it was survival, and it was love in action.

When my dad found out, he told me, "You're scraping the bottom of the barrel. That's not who I raised you to be."

That comment stuck and for a long time, it felt like confirmation that I had failed—that I wasn't living up to whatever invisible metric he still held over me.

Then, a few years later, I told that story to a friend. She looked at me completely flabbergasted and said, "What do you mean that's not who he raised you to be? He isn't proud you are a survivor and someone who is willing to take in a teenager and give her safety and a fresh start?"

That reframe cracked something open. I realized that I had spent most of my life chasing someone else's definition of success—one that kept moving—and calling myself a failure when I couldn't reach it.

What I've learned since then is this: it's impossible to live up to someone else's standards and still be a happy, functioning human.

We often treat failure as a verdict—the final word—when in truth it's usually someone else's measurement. What if it's not an ending at all? What if failure is just the moment we realize we've been running toward the wrong ruler?

Let's explore that idea—and how we can learn to counteract it.

The Stories We Believe About Failure

There's a story most of us learned long before we understood success:

> *If you fail, you're not good enough.*
>
> *Not:*
>
> *"That didn't work, try again."*
>
> *"That strategy wasn't the right fit."*
>
> *"The timing wasn't aligned."*

No — the way we were raised, failure became a stamp of identity.

It wasn't:

> *"You failed at that thing."*

It became:

> *"You are a failure."*

And that programmed belief has shaped every risk we take; every idea we hold back, every goal we secretly want but don't claim out loud.

The First Stories

We learn how capable we are from the voices around us:

> *Parents grading our dreams*
>
> *Teachers ranking our abilities*
>
> *Coaches measuring our performance*
>
> *Friends teasing our attempts*

A world obsessed with outcomes

For many of us, approval became the ultimate currency.

We traded authenticity for applause.

We traded curiosity for correctness.

We traded courage for safety.

Because if we never take big swings… we never have to face big falls.

I've had many coaches in my sports history, some good, some bad, and one that is unforgettable.

You can stand out from a pack in a variety of ways. I made it a habit as much as possible not to be noticed. I wasn't a very confident teenager and didn't always feel like I fit in with my team. One day at practice during a timed drill where we swung at a fake pitch, dropped the bat, and ran to first, Coach asked us who was the fastest getting to first base. Lindsey was the overwhelming favorite guess and we were all wrong.

I was the fastest on the team running to first base.

From that day on my job was to hit a ground ball to the short stop and beat the throw to first. And I did. Every time. I am nothing if not an executor of clear expectations. You would think this would have shored me up, but I wasn't in a place to recognize that job as important nor my ability to do it as successful.

At 16 all I saw was the high fives and hugs for the high profile plays. I never was recognized as an MVP nor was "Chani made first base 4 times in last night's game" ever announced on the loudspeaker the same way a double or home run was announced in the game recap. My job may have been important to the coach, but it was a silent one.

One game I did hit a triple. Our opponents at this point were used to me grounding to the short stop so the outfield moved in. I connected with a perfect pitch and sailed that ball into left field, right over the outstretched gloves of the outfielders. I stopped on third base elated that I was going to be recognized and celebrated.

And I was, but not in the way I anticipated.

Coach lectured me on how lucky I was that the outfield moved in. Told me how risky that move was and that I can let the team down by not doing my job.

The risk I took that made me feel so good was not worth it to him. On that team I would never be more than a silent single hit to first base. Quiet and dependable.

 **Power Pause**

Think of a moment when someone else's definition of success made you feel small. Whose bar were you trying to reach? What would happen if you stopped measuring yourself by it?

The Myth of Finality

Growing up, we are silently taught:

Good = perfect

Failure = humiliation

Mistakes = weakness

Trying hard but not winning = embarrassing

So we learn to hide the learning process by pretending we know everything, striving for flawlessness because we fear judgement more that we fear stagnation.

Somewhere along the way...progress became terrifying. Why is this? Progress means trying, trying invites mistakes, and mistakes risk criticism.

For most of us, the word failure feels like a full stop. We fail the test, miss the promotion, lose the client, drop the ball—and our inner voice declares, "That's it. I'm not cut out for this." That feeling of finality is the real myth. Failure isn't the period at the end of your story; it's the comma that forces you to take a breath and choose the next sentence.

Psychologist Carol Dweck calls this the growth mindset: the belief that our abilities aren't fixed but expandable. When we treat mistakes as data instead of verdicts, we stay curious—and curiosity is what drives mastery.

I used to think my dad's voice was preparing me for the "real world." Maybe it did—because I became excellent at anticipating criticism. But it also made me allergic to risk. It took years of falling flat—on sales calls, marketing attempts, even friendships—to realize that every so-called failure was actually feedback.

The truth is, failure doesn't decide your worth. It simply offers evidence of what happens when you stretch beyond your comfort zone. It's proof that you were in motion.

When we redefine failure as information instead of identity, we remove its power to shame us. And once the shame loses its hold, growth can finally begin.

Power Pause

Think about something you've labeled a failure—a project, a conversation, a relationship. What if you rewrote the sentence to say, "This experience taught me _______"? Fill in that blank and notice how the story shifts.

How Fear of Failure Shapes Women

Somewhere along the way, women were handed an invisible rulebook that says:

Be ambitious, but don't seem too aggressive.

Be confident, but not arrogant.

Be nurturing, but never needy.

Be excellent, but never exhausted.

We learn early that the world claps loudest for our success stories and whispers during our struggles. Because the whispers sting, we avoid them. That's how fear of failure quietly takes root—it's not just the fear of getting it wrong; it's the fear of being seen getting it wrong.

Research shows women report higher perfectionism and self-criticism than men, especially in leadership. When we make a mistake, we don't just evaluate the outcome—we question our entire identity.

We replay the losses:

The relationship that ended

The goal missed by inches

The business idea that didn't take off

The moment we froze instead of rising

The time we quit because it hurt too much

We become historians of our own shortcomings and we archive every loss as evidence against ourselves.

I can think of a dozen moments when fear kept me small: hesitating to pitch collaborations, sitting on ideas too long, rewriting one email three times so I wouldn't look unprofessional.

Sound familiar?

Fear of failure makes even capable women shrink to fit inside someone else's comfort zone. We stay busy instead of bold, make plans instead of moves, and ask permission instead of trusting ourselves.

But fear doesn't fade by waiting for perfect conditions. It shrinks when we act anyway - when we take one messy, brave step and survive it. On the other side of every "failure" you feared is quiet proof that you're stronger than the story you told yourself.

Failure doesn't prove your limit. Failure reveals where your growth begins. It isn't a verdict, it's information.

 **Power Pause**

Where are you still playing safe because you're afraid of being seen as failing? What one small, courageous step could you take this week—even if it's imperfect?

Reclaiming the Narrative

When you hear a voice saying:

> *"You can't do that."*
>
> *"You're not ready."*
>
> *"That's not good enough."*

Whose voice is it?

Failure takes the voice of my father and it's rooted in childhood. I was always expected to be calm, quiet, and tractable. To be honest, I don't remember a lot of my early childhood. Mid to late-childhood I remember spending a lot of time reading and doing puzzles when I was home and as much time away from home as I could. In my experience, that limited the criticism and therefore the feeling of failure.

Somewhere between "try your best" and "never let them see you fail," we lost the middle ground—the part where learning actually happens. Why is this?

Instead of cheering bravery…we critique the landing.

So we avoid the jump.

We avoid the attempt.

We avoid the risk.

Not because we doubt the dream — but because we dread the judgment.

Power Pause

Write one thing you stopped pursuing because someone made you feel like you weren't good enough.

Would you try again if judgment wasn't a factor?

For years, I equated failure with shame. But after enough disappointments, I noticed a pattern: every so-called "failure" had taught me something I could never have learned from success.

The first time I hosted a workshop, only three people showed up. I was frustrated because I had worked hard on my presentation. But when I looked back, I realized that day was a gift. It forced me to practice, to refine, to prepare for what came next. That "failed" event gave me courage to build the community I have now.

This is what failing with flying colors looks like—the art of letting experience be the teacher instead of the judge.

Researcher Brené Brown calls this the rumble—the vulnerable space where we face truth without pretending it's pretty. "Vulnerability," she says, "is having the courage to show up when you can't control the outcome."

When we stop editing out the messy parts, our story shifts from "I failed" to "I learned." The moment we claim our lessons, we reclaim our power.

Failure stops being a wound and starts becoming a witness: I've been there. I grew. I survived.

Power Pause

List three lessons that came from things that didn't work out. How did each one strengthen you—skills, boundaries, clarity? Take a moment to honor that growth.

Permission to Reframe

Let's rewrite the definition:

> *Failure is simply a moment when reality reveals what needs to shift.*

When a plan doesn't go the way you hoped?

> *That's guidance.*

When a goal takes longer than expected?

> *That's pacing.*

When something falls apart?

> *That's redirection.*

You are not failing – you are learning your way through.

Failure is not a verdict, a measure of your worth, nor is it a character flaw. Recognize failure for what it is:

> *Information*
>
> *A feedback loop*
>
> *A clue to what matters*

A sign you are moving

Proof that you are trying something that stretches you

Failure is not the end — it is the middle of any real story.

Turning Points: From Shame to Strategy

Failure keeps its grip only when we leave it unexamined. Once we look at it with curiosity, shame dissolves and wisdom remains.

Most of the time, we aren't afraid of the thing not working.

We're afraid of:

- What people will think
- What people will say
- How we'll look
- Who might be disappointed
- Whether they'll be right about us

Failure feels dangerous because pride, identity, and dreams are exposed. Here's the twist - if you're afraid you might fail, it means you're trying something that matters.

You don't fear falling from the chair you're sitting in. You fear falling when you're reaching for something higher.

Fear is a signal — not a stop sign.

Fill in this sentence: "I'm not afraid of failing at ____________________. I'm afraid people will think ____________________."

Where is the fear actually pointing you?

Failing With Flying Colors — The Quiet Wins

I used to replay my mistakes on a loop. Every missed opportunity, every awkward conversation. But replaying isn't reviewing. One keeps you stuck in guilt; the other moves you forward.

When I started reviewing my failures like a coach instead of a critic, everything changed. That's when I instituted a Failure Debrief—a simple four-step process I still use whenever something doesn't go as planned.

1. *What Happened? State the facts without judgment.*
2. *What Did I Feel? Name the emotions; naming softens them.*
3. *What Did I Learn? Pull out the insight.*
4. *What Will I Do Next Time? Turn the lesson into strategy.*

The first time I used this was after a networking event that flopped spectacularly. Only two people came, one left early, and the coffee maker broke. Instead of saying I failed, I debriefed: my marketing was vague, the date conflicted with another event, and I had tied my worth to attendance. Once I separated the lesson from the label, I felt in control again.

Failure doesn't shrink us; unexamined shame does. When we face setbacks with curiosity, we turn "never again" into "next time."

If our failures clarify what we want, show who supports us, and build resilience within us they are no longer setbacks. They become lessons in what no longer works, help us evolve strategy, and grow our courage.

Each "failure" you've ever felt? It didn't push you backward. It pushed you forward differently. Every time something didn't go your way, you gained more tools for the next attempt. You don't need fewer failures. You need more untamed, unapologetic tries.

Let me say that again louder:

You Need More UNTAMED, UNAPOLOGETIC TRIES!

Power Pause

Pick one recent stumble and walk it through the four steps of the Failure Debrief. What surprised you? What will you do differently next time?

Journal Exercise – Your Failure-to-Fuel Framework

Every woman who has built something real has failed her way forward. The difference isn't the absence of failure—it's what she does with it.

You've unpacked the old scripts; now rewrite them.

Step 1: Rewrite the Story - Retell a "failure" using the language of learning. Name the gift inside it.

Step 2: Extract the Wisdom - List three truths that experience taught you about who you are and what matters.

Step 3: Take the Next Right Step - Choose one small action that reflects your new understanding.

Step 4: Share It - Tell your redefined-failure story to someone else. Speaking it breaks shame and spreads courage.

 **Power Pause**

Take a moment to breathe and recognize how far you've come. You're not just reading—you're rebuilding. You are living proof that failure is fuel.

Closing Reflection

Let's rewrite your relationship with failure because you are not defined by what didn't work.

> *You are defined by your willingness to rise again.*
>
> *You've gathered evidence that you're growing faster than your comfort zone can keep up.*
>
> *Every stumble and every "not yet" is feedback guiding you closer to alignment.*

From here forward, you will not let failure shrink you. You will let failure shape you.

In the next chapter, we'll move from redefining failure to redefining success—building a vision that fits your life, your values, and your energy by reclaiming who you are without the hustle.

Success isn't a destination; it's the rhythm you create when you stop apologizing for evolving.

Chapter 3: Who Am I Without the Hustle

The Identity Crisis We Didn't See Coming

Many women don't realize how deeply they've tied their self-worth to output until the moment they are forced to stop:

- A health crisis
- A burnout crash
- A baby on the way
- A caregiving role
- A global shutdown
- A schedule disruption that derails everything

Suddenly…the hustle isn't available anymore. And what's left?

Exhaustion.

Fear.

Emptiness.

A sense of invisibility.

Because if the world stops needing us…do we still matter?

Power Pause

When was the last time you stopped moving long enough to notice who you are without your to-do list? What came up — peace or panic?

The Cult of Busyness

We live in a world that worships the hustle. Society celebrates the woman who "does it all" — the entrepreneur who's up before dawn, the mom who runs on coffee and calendar invites, the boss who never takes a day off.

Busyness has become a status symbol, proof that we matter. But here's the truth: exhaustion is not a badge of honor and too many women I know wear it as one.

A 2022 Deloitte Women @ Work study found that 53% of working women report feeling burned out — and most of them feel pressure to hide it. That means half of us are running on empty while pretending to be fine.

The constant grind gives us a temporary high — that dopamine rush of checking the next box, sending the next email, conquering the next goal. But it's short-lived. Before long, the silence between achievements starts to feel like failure.

We start to believe that if we slow down, the world will forget us.

But here's the secret: the world doesn't reward speed; it rewards substance.

We have an identity beyond our output.

Before we learned productivity, before we learned we were valuable because of a list of accomplishments, there was a sense of joy and wonder and simply existing.

In my search to rediscover myself I have done a lot of personality assessments, energy classes to determine my productive hours, and what seems like endless self-help books. Imposter syndrome rears its ugly head still, but I know I am meant to be where I am and doing what I am doing. I just need to remember there is a cost to the constant race.

The cost comes in missed family moments, friends who stop reaching out, postponed joy, and disconnection from your partner. You and I have the power to choose – we can choose not to hustle through our whole lives only to look back and realize we missed it.

Power Pause

Write down three things you often brag or joke about being "too busy" for. What might life look like if you stopped treating those as badges of honor?

The Fear of Stillness

Stillness can feel terrifying when your identity is built on motion.

Many of us learned that rest must be earned — after the house is clean, after the inbox is empty, after everyone else is taken care of. The problem is, those boxes never stay checked.

Sometimes when I try to rest, I feel fidgety. My brain immediately starts scanning for what I "should" be doing instead. That's not failure; that's physiology. When your nervous system has been trained to live in fight-or-flight mode, calm feels foreign.

> *"I can't slow down — I'll have a panic attack."*
>
> *"I can't stop moving because my brain won't slow down."*

I can't even count the number of years that was my everyday truth.

I thought I thrived in fight-or-flight mode — always moving, always doing, forgetting to eat, never stopping to breathe or enjoy.

It felt like failure to stop.

There was a very real fear that if I dropped one ball or took even a moment away from my responsibilities, I'd let someone down or something catastrophic would happen.

But the truth is, we can only be in so many places at once.

So why did my calendar have me in two or three places in the same hour?

Flitting between events and activities meant I was never truly present. I was watching the clock, already planning my next move.

I remember one year in college when I would literally lie awake at night, stressing because there were dishes left undone in the sink. That hasn't completely gone away, but I've learned to accept that not everything gets 100% done 100% of the time.

And you know what? My house hasn't exploded.

My son has never said, "Mama, you didn't schedule enough meetings this week."

Could I set higher goals for my business and spend even more time working? Absolutely. But that would throw me right back into the cycle I've worked so hard to break.

I don't want to spend every waking moment in my business.

I have a family, friends — and I want to create time for me.

Which brings up another truth: I had to figure out who I was again once I finally slowed down.

> *Did I still enjoy the same hobbies?*
>
> *Did I still value the same principles?*

I had been moving for so long that I didn't even know what still fit.

But rest isn't laziness. It's recalibration. It's your body whispering, "You can't pour from an empty cup, and you don't have to."

When we resist rest, we're not protecting our ambition — we're starving it. Stillness creates the clarity that hustle keeps us too distracted to find.

Power Pause

When you imagine slowing down, what's the first uncomfortable thought that shows up? ("I'll fall behind"? "People will think I'm lazy"?) Write it down. What would happen if that belief wasn't true?

Rediscovering the Self Beneath the Schedule

Who are you when you take away the titles?

For years, I introduced myself as what I did — business owner, mother, mentor, organizer. It felt natural because those roles were the easiest way to explain my value. But those are things I do, not who I am.

When I started asking myself, "Who am I without the hustle?" the first answers that surfaced were uncomfortable silence. It took time to remember that I'm also curious, creative, funny, and compassionate — things that don't depend on productivity.

The truth is, we've spent so long building resumes that we've forgotten how to build relationships — with ourselves.

Stopping reveals things we've been running from - our unmet needs, our neglected emotions, and our disconnection from joy. The truth about how tired we are.

Hustle has a side effect: it erases identity outside of achievement.

> *Ask a woman what she does for fun… and she might not know anymore.*
>
> *Ask her what she loves about herself… and she may pause longer than makes sense.*
>
> *Ask her who she is when she isn't performing… and she can't answer.*

For many years I gave up my hobbies. I am pretty sure I forgot what they were because I not only wasn't giving myself time to do them, I wasn't giving myself time to think about them. Do you realize I have yarn I bought before I moved to Texas in 2006?

The reality is there are many enjoyable things that don't actually take a lot of time or a lot of money to do. If I was prioritizing myself I would have taken a few minutes a day to work on a knitting project instead of leaving it in the bin.

I've learned that some of my greatest ideas come when my body is moving - whether it's my hands or my feet. That part of my brain that spirals down the rabbit hole of what isn't done gets quiet if I'm doing something. It seems to tame the fight or flight mode. Being lost in the constant need to hustle occupied 100% of my brain and my time for years.

Reconnecting with who you are beneath the schedule is an act of rebellion. It's saying, I am enough, even when I'm not producing.

 **Power Pause**

List five words that describe you without referencing your job, your family, or your accomplishments. Who is that woman? What does she love? What does she need?

The Gentle Power of Rest and Receptivity

Rest isn't weakness — it's wisdom.

When we slow down, we stop reacting and start receiving. Inspiration, creativity, and intuition live in the quiet spaces we've been taught to fear.

The science backs it up: when your brain rests, it consolidates information, repairs connections, and makes space for innovation. That's why your best ideas show up in the shower or on a walk, not when you're glued to your laptop at 11 pm.

And truth is that sometimes our bodies just call "Time Out".

I've had a few wake-up calls at different points in my life. One of the biggest came when I was managing a restaurant.

I was forty years old and pregnant — and I knew nothing about pregnancy. Especially about being Old and Pregnant (you older Moms know exactly what I mean). My body was sending every signal that something wasn't right: vision loss, pain in my hips, exhaustion beyond anything I'd ever felt. Around twenty-six weeks in, I started having sharp lower abdominal pain.

I was working forty to fifty hours a week on my feet, managing a team, solving everyone else's problems, and ignoring my own. The people around me complained when I couldn't keep up. My doctor told me that if I didn't want to work, I'd have to talk to my husband about it.

At twenty-eight weeks pregnant, I was in the emergency room for what they thought was a cardiac event. They admitted me and while I was cleared of the cardiac event, I was diagnosed with HELLP syndrome. My liver and kidneys were shutting down and they found polyps in my gall bladder that could be cancerous. My blood pressure was too high and I was put on medication to stop contractions. After two days, I was sent home and a specialist was called in to help coordinate my care.

At thirty weeks, I had an emergency C-section because my son wasn't getting enough blood through the umbilical cord. We were both in danger of dying at this point.

Full stop.

My body had had enough. My years of training in how not to stop had finally caught up with me.

Four weeks after giving birth to my son, I had a tubal ligation and my gallbladder removed. Eight weeks later, I was back at work full time. Not long after, I became the General Manager — working seventy hours a week or more. I kept that up for two years.

During that time, I was diagnosed with postpartum depression and PTSD. I had no real relationship with my son. I was moving and working to avoid thinking and feeling.

And then one day, I was done.

I went home and told my husband I was stepping down, buying chickens, and baking bread. Yup — he thought I was nuts. 42 chickens and a curated book of recipes later, *Chicken Rita Baked Goods* was born.

For a while, it was blissfully simple. I spent four days a week resting and being with my family, and three days baking and selling goods at farmers markets. I'd nap while things were in the oven on night two, and stay awake all of night one.

Notice something? I was still not in a sustainable pattern. Eventually, I tore a muscle in my abdomen — and life came to a stop again. At some point, our bodies simply can't keep up.

Since then, I've been learning to listen to mine. I still bring my laptop home most nights, planning to work after everyone goes to bed. But lately? I've been falling asleep first.

And you know what? That's okay.

I've had to adjust my schedule, pay closer attention to what tasks actually matter, and learn to take breaks throughout the day. I can do more in fewer productive hours than I ever did in endless, frantic ones.

For example, between 2-3pm every day my brain shuts down and sometimes my body does too. For years my answer was caffeine. At one point I was drinking multiple 200mg caffeine energy drinks in a day combined with coffee or soda. My doctor said lay off the energy drinks or they'll kill me.

I got lots of advice on how to avoid this afternoon slump. I found that getting exercise, eating more protein, and actually staying hydrated have helped with the body fatigue. But I'm also 47 and perimenopausal (that's a whole other book) and the brain fog doesn't stop.

I learned to focus my tasks into my most effective hours. Now when that brain slump hits, I embrace it. I might walk, I might nap or meditate, or I might do some reading. It's rare that I try to power through, but if I have to be working, I do research or admin tasks that are not client facing. My clients, family, and friends need me at my best. If you have ever talked to me at 8am and 2pm you know I have a very different attitude and tone of voice.

When I'm rested, I'm focused. When I'm focused, I'm effective.

And when I stop chasing the clock, I finally get to live my life inside it.

I used to think that stepping away would set me back. What I learned is that rest doesn't erase progress — it strengthens it. Every time I pause, I come back more focused, more intentional, more aligned.

You don't lose ground when you rest. You grow roots.

Power Pause

Where can you create white space this week — ten minutes, an hour, or a day — to do absolutely nothing productive? Notice the resistance. What does it tell you about your relationship with rest?

Journal Exercise – Reclaiming Your Worth Without the Work

You were not born to prove yourself through productivity. You were born to create, connect, and contribute from a place of wholeness.

Let's practice remembering that.

I Am Worthy Even When ______________________________.

Complete the sentence five times - examples below

I am worthy even when I rest.

I am worthy even when I say no.

I am worthy even when I'm not achieving.

Schedule a Pause.

Pick one day or one hour this week to stop hustling. Turn off the noise. Breathe. Be.

Reflect Without Judgment.

Journal what you noticed — guilt, relief, clarity, joy — and thank yourself for showing up differently.

You are not the hustle. You are the heartbeat that drives it. When you slow down, your power doesn't fade — it focuses.

Power Pause

What truth do you most want to remember from this chapter? Write it down somewhere you'll see it when life starts to speed up again.

Closing Reflection — You Still Deserve to Exist

You are not your inbox.

You are not your revenue.

You are not your to-do list.

Your importance does not decrease when you rest.

Your identity does not disappear when you slow down.

Your worth does not vanish when you pause.

You are allowed to simply be.

In the next chapter, we begin the shift and release the guilt. We will build success on our own terms.

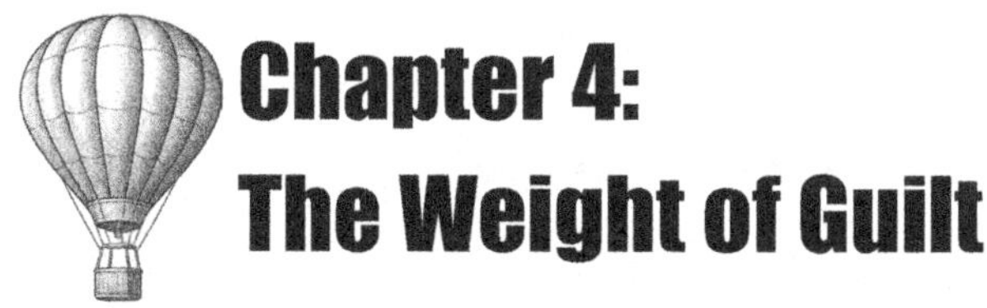

Chapter 4: The Weight of Guilt

Guilt, Front and Center

You are carrying guilt that isn't yours to hold.

And it's heavy — body-heavy, soul-heavy, anxiety-heavy.

Because the math never makes sense:

> *If you work too much → you're a bad mom.*
>
> *If you work too little → you're a bad business owner.*
>
> *If you take time for yourself → you're selfish.*
>
> *If you don't → you're exhausted, resentful, and still guilty.*

Guilt always shows up like it pays rent. She's like a toddler (and most husbands) - loud, dramatic, and very bad at minding her own business.

Power Pause

Where does guilt show up first for you — in your chest, your stomach, or your thoughts?

Circle the answer that feels true right now.

The Double Bind

Here's the impossible game women are handed:

Be fully present for your family.

Be fully committed to your business.

Be fully available to everyone you love.

Be fully rested and glowing.

Be fully selfless and also self-actualized.

Be everything… everywhere… all at once.

And if you drop even one of those expectations? Cue the guilt soundtrack. On repeat.

We weren't designed to succeed under those rules. We were set up to feel like we're failing — no matter what we choose. Guilt isn't proof that you are doing something wrong. It's proof that you care. The women who worry about failing are usually the ones holding everything together.

Journal Exercise

Finish the sentence:

"If I'm a great mom, I must be _______________ in my business."

"If I'm great in my business, I must be _____________ as a mom."

Where did these beliefs come from?

Do you even agree with them?

A Story from the Middle of the Mess

I can't even count the number of times guilt convinced me I was dropping all the balls.

If I missed a school event for a client meeting, I felt like the worst mom in the world.

If I skipped out on an opportunity to be with my son, I felt like the worst business owner.

And if I tried to sneak in 30 minutes of peace? Oh, guilt had PLENTY to say about that.

There were days I would beat myself up for choosing the "wrong" priority — even though both mattered to me. Even though I was doing everything I could.

This is a hard thing to change. The feeling of guilt still creeps in. I didn't always recognize it at first. I would feel overwhelmed and restless and unable to pinpoint what I could do to relieve that feeling. Yelling at my husband didn't help. Trying to push through work when I was angry and unfocused didn't help. Exercise did help – but you can only pace the hallways so many times.

I had to get in a new routine overall. I had to realize that the angry restless feeling of not doing enough was really me trying to do too much. My son can't get quality time if I come home in work mode. Work wouldn't let me rest because my To Do List was never done.

I'll let you in on a little secret – my To Do List will never be done. It's impossible. What I focus on is a prioritized list each day of what is most important. I block off time on my calendar to focus on it. If it's not time to be thinking about it, I don't think about it. Calendar time vs stuck in my head time. It is easy to be consumed and feel like you are failing all. the. time.

The soundtrack likes to play on repeat, but you can change the CD. Try being intentional with your thoughts and energy. Are your most important work tasks done before you get home at night? Then put that phone on silent. Shut that laptop and be present for friends and family. Show up for you. If you aren't feeling guilty about work, could you enjoy a book or a drink with friends? Play in the park with your children?

If you aren't feeling that nauseous, sinking feeling of dread of what isn't done, what would you feel instead? Listen, this shift isn't instant and it isn't easy. It requires practice and intention. Remember to celebrate progress over perfection. It's easy to slip into old habits. There are also times that require you to focus more energy either at work or at home.

The important thing is to give yourself the same grace you give everyone else. If your partner or friend came to you and said they were struggling with guilt and feeling like they weren't enough, what would you tell them? How would you address their feelings of failure?

I challenge you to turn the tables and use those words for yourself. I'm learning to communicate with my husband when I am drive mode at work for a deadline or large project. Instead of yelling at him for not helping, I tell him what he can do to relieve some of my burden. Let's be real – people aren't mind readers. They don't know what you need unless you tell them. It was a hard lesson for me to learn that the yelling I was doing wasn't because I was angry with him, it's because I felt like I was failing.

 **Power Pause**

Write down a moment from the past week where guilt tried to tell you you were failing.

What was actually true in that moment?

Guilt's Favorite Trick: "You Should..."

Research has a name for this: The Mental Load — and women carry the majority of it.

> *Planning.*
>
> *Preparing.*
>
> *Remembering.*

Emotional stability management for the whole household.

Let's face it, we all have about sixteen tabs open in our brain cataloging what we forgot to put on the shopping list, which family member has a doctor's appointment when, who needs a ride where, and did we send that email or is it still in the draft folder? We are trying our best to keep up with all of the work nobody sees and the jobs we don't get paid for.

There are a million "I should" thoughts clamoring for priority. It can become a litany of our shame. The voice of our critic categorizing our failures. We struggle until we explode or shut down. Who here has ever taken a long shower just to cry? Sat in the car in your driveway dreading going into the house because you are already exhausted and you know a million things need to be done? Knowing that people still need your time and attention.

You give and give and give every day, and yet guilt tells you you're still not doing enough.

Here's what's true:

> *Guilt is often just internalized expectation — someone else's voice wearing your tone.*

You're not guilty.

You're tired.

Power Pause

Which voice is your guilt using?

> *A parent from childhood*
>
> *A boss from a past job*
>
> *Social media "perfect moms"*
>
> *Your own impossible standards*

Name it → and its power shrinks.

Choosing Without Apology

Here's the most freeing truth of this chapter:

> *Your choices don't need to be justified to anyone.*

You're not choosing work over family or family over ambition or self over responsibility.

On a day that goes according to plan, I drop my son off at school and arrive at the office or my first meeting. My most critical items get checked off, a fire may get put out, and I pick my son up from school. We have dinner and go through our nightly routine. After he falls asleep my husband and I try to find time to connect with each other or watch a show.

You may have noticed there wasn't anything in that list that was me doing something for me. As women we are naturally nurturers and it's so so easy to put ourselves last.

If I go too long without doing something for myself I shut down and disappear into a book for hours while life happens around me or I struggle to remain focused during work hours. I become cranky and less productive.

I have had to learn to take that mental step back around the 2pm hour that I mentioned earlier. Sometimes I will get up an hour before my family to drink a cup of coffee in silence. Once or twice a month I take myself out for lunch and disconnect for an hour. Getting in a workout routine helps – and let me tell you, mine isn't strenuous. It's quick and easy and I can do it in my office. Because if it didn't check those boxes it wouldn't get done.

Remember progress over perfection. Do not compare yourself to other people. You do not owe anyone an explanation for your choices. As long as you are moving the needle forward each day in your business and in your personal life you will hit the success mark you set for yourself. We have to stop chasing what other people choose for us.

The expectation may be for me to never stop grinding until I hit my goal. It's my choice not to. I am not a marathon runner; I am a sprinter. When I acknowledge that and break my tasks into smaller chunks allowing for some downtime, I can still get to goal. If I push too hard in the beginning and tap out at mile 20 I have chosen to let down myself and those who depend on me.

Prioritize some time for yourself. We have all heard you can't pour from an empty cup. I encourage you to pick up an empty cup and pour that water right over your head. Can't do it, can you? It seems silly, but if you ever need to remind yourself to fill your cup, literally try to pour from an empty one.

You may have to make some decisions and sacrifices when you start prioritizing. That's ok. You will make choices in the moment that are important to you and your peace.

Harsh reality is that sometimes choosing feels like betrayal. If you choose to prioritize work, family feels sacrificed. If you choose to prioritize family, ambition feels sacrificed. Let's reframe choice – instead of choosing against something, try choosing for something.

Every day you will make decisions – big ones, small ones, heart-tugging ones. Guilt will try to twist every choice into a loss – a failure. Only people with purpose have to make tough calls. Choosing isn't a betrayal, it's leadership.

Power Pause

Practice this sentence:

"This is what my life needs from me right now — and that is enough."

Say it out loud.

Let it land.

Self-Respect Over Self-Sacrifice

Women are praised for sacrifice… and punished for boundaries.

Many of us have been raised to believe that the highest form of love is sacrifice. We were taught to quiet our voices, carry the load without complaint, and put everyone else's needs before our own. It wasn't just our families; it was the rulebook society handed us through textbooks, advice columns and invisible expectations.

Research shows this isn't just noble — it's costly. A comprehensive review found that women who engage in chronic self-silencing — suppressing their thoughts, feelings or needs — face significantly greater risks of depression, eating disorders, and even cardiovascular disease. (Maji & Dixit, 2019) And a landmark study of over 300 mid-life women found that higher self-silencing was associated with increased odds of carotid plaque — a marker of cardiovascular disease — independent of depression and traditional risk factors. (Jakubowski et al., 2022)

At the same time, feminist ethics scholars point out that the ideal of the endlessly-giving woman has been structurally embedded: care ethics often celebrates self-sacrifice while treating self-respect as optional. (Cawston & Archer, 2018)

Here's the truth you're going to carry: Self-respect is not the opposite of love. It's the foundation of love. You cannot give what you don't have. You cannot protect what you've sacrificed into depletion. And you cannot lead from the margin if you've depleted your voice and your body.

So today, when you feel that familiar tug of guilt — the voice that says "I must do more" or "I didn't do enough" — pause. Ask:

> *"Am I giving out of joy or out of fear?"*

Because guilt is not a compass. It won't lead you toward the life you want, it will keep you in the life you were told to want.

So here's the new rule:

If guilt is the only reason you're saying yes — the answer is no.

You are allowed to protect:

Your time

Your energy

Your peace

Your joy

Your family

Your business

You

I spent most of my life people pleasing. And I admit that I still struggle with this. My first instinct is to say "Yes" and then find a way to do whatever it is to make life easier for the requester. It caused so much internal strife as I found myself overextended again and again. Work and family continued to be out of balance and sometimes both ended up on the back burner. For a long time I couldn't say "No" because guilt consumed me. I knew my needs weren't as important as theirs and I continued in a cycle of devaluing myself.

It wasn't until recently that I started looking at requests from other people through a lens that allowed me to see what impact fulfilling their need would have on me. How much of my time and energy will it take? Do I have time available without sacrificing something already planned? Will helping them keep me aligned with my goals and values? Will it make me feel good helping or will it cause stress and anxiety? Is there someone better suited I can refer them to?

I have established more boundaries and less people are calling me. The truth? Those calls were draining. The fact that they aren't calling now means they only wanted to take what I could give them and they weren't bringing anything to fill my cup.

Own your boundary:

- *Write one boundary you will enforce this week without apology.*
- *Write one NO you will allow yourself—simply because you choose it.*
- *Write one "yes" you owe yourself because you believe you deserve it.*

You do not owe anyone your depletion to prove your devotion.

You don't have to explain your boundaries.

You don't have to diminish your success or soften your ambition.

You don't have to sacrifice your self-respect for someone else's comfort.

Journal Exercise — Release the Charge

Whenever guilt hits, ask three questions:

1. *Is this guilt or conditioning?*
2. *Does this choice reflect my values?*
3. *If a woman I love were in this position, would I judge her?*

Think about the last moment guilt hit. Work through your feelings here.

Closing Reflection — The New Truth

Guilt doesn't get to drive anymore.

You are building a life that honors all parts of you — not just the parts the world finds convenient.

You are allowed to rise without apologizing for the view.

You are allowed to choose without explaining the math.

You are allowed to love your work and love your people and love yourself…without guilt scoring the points.

This life you're building? It's yours.

And you're allowed to enjoy it.

Next we'll look at how to sustain the alignment we are building beginning with how we define success.

UR-SKI

Chapter 5: Redefining Success

The Definition Shift

For so many women success has looked like sacrificing sleep to get more done, saying yes to everything, hitting milestones no matter the cost, and achieving goals we are too tired to celebrate.

Success used to be a checklist.

✓ *More clients.*

✓ *More income.*

✓ *More recognition.*

I was chasing all the "mores," yet I still went to bed feeling behind. I was still living someone else's version of achievement and measuring my happiness by metrics that don't make me happy.

Then one day, I caught myself standing in front of the mirror blankly staring. 200% exhausted and wondering why I looked so miserable when I have so much to be grateful for.

That was my wake-up call. I realized I'd achieved someone else's version of success — polished, productive, but not mine. That moment changed everything.

My Turning Point

My turning point came during the third year of my Financial Services Practice. I have a contract goal that sets my minimum measure of success — and technically, the sky's the limit.

I'd watch other agents in my office pull in over a million dollars in commissions. Many were earning six figures all day long.

It felt like a struggle I couldn't win and a mountain I couldn't climb to keep up with them.

Why? Because I was focused on the end result — the commission total. My constant thought was, I can't achieve that. I doubted whether I was even in the right industry. I tried to fit myself into a mold that didn't fit me.

Here's a shocker: I am not a white male in a suit with a membership card to the Good Old Boys Club. My industry is changing, but historically, that's what people have looked for — and that's the image I thought I had to emulate to be seen as successful.

Women, though, don't have a long history of financial freedom. And we often carry a heavier load.

We don't get to wear one hat — we wear all of them. We clean, cook, raise children, care for aging parents, manage households, and run businesses.

Men are wonderful, but let's face it — in most homes, women still do the heavy lifting.

Why We Chase the Wrong Wins

Growing up we learned:

> *Success = Praise*
>
> *Failure = Rejection*

We trained ourselves to be whatever earned approval and if something felt misaligned, we assumed we were the problem. I'll ask you again here – whose idea of success are you chasing and does it make you feel fulfilled?

How many days do you spend saying things like:

> *"I should be grateful"*
>
> *"I should be further by now"*
>
> *"I should be stronger"*
>
> *"I should be more"*

For me, that is a measuring stick of everything I am not living up to. It's unrealistic and damaging.

If we can unlearn the fear of rejection and take the word "should" out of our vocabulary, what power can we start to wield over our own success?

I began to shift my measurement of success. Instead of chasing commissions, I started asking myself: Is my house comfortable? Is my family happy? Do I feel like I'm making a difference for my clients?

Now, I focus on working with clients who value what I bring — people whose lives I can genuinely impact. My success is measured in the level of trust my clients place in me, the number of relationships I build vs products sold.

Wins for me are the messages that say:

> *"I am so grateful for your help."*
>
> *"You took a convoluted concept and broke it down in such an easy to understand way."*
>
> *"You are one of the few people I feel isn't trying to take advantage of me."*
>
> *"My kids need to talk to you. I'll bring you over to meet them."*

My production slowed while I made a shift in my business, but I feel better. My clients are getting better service. And my family? They are getting home cooked meals again and cooking is something I enjoy.

That feels like success to me.

 **Power Pause**

Think of a time you achieved something others envied, yet it didn't satisfy you. What did that experience reveal about what success truly means to you?

Success by Someone Else's Rules

From childhood, we're handed templates for success:

> *Good grades.*
>
> *Stable job.*
>
> *Marriage, mortgage, milestones.*

Then, in entrepreneurship, we trade those for new templates:

Six-figure years.

Five-step funnels.

Endless growth.

But the rules are the same — they measure output, not alignment.

We forget that achievement without alignment is just acceleration in the wrong direction.

It's so easy to look good on the outside. We carefully curate our image — our social-media posts, advertisements, memberships. People tell me they've seen my magazine ad and say, "Business must be booming!" And sometimes, it is. More often, I'm burning the candle at both ends, wondering why my insides don't line up with my outsides.

It gets measured in words like "Mama just has to send this one email" that spiral into an hour. It's the moment I cancel a prospect meeting because the admin tasks are piling up and my body is exhausted from tossing and turning the night before. Do I meet someone when I'm not at my best, or do I prioritize myself and say, "Hey, that's too much — it's okay to step back in this moment."

The internal war we wage against ourselves, our calendar, and our guilt is exhausting. No one sees it.

Though sometimes I wonder — the people I look to as "successful," do their insides match their outsides?

We are measuring output, and the world is judging us on the output. But how much farther could we go if we aligned with what feels right for us? What if we decide that success is not about being "the best." Can you imagine if your success is about living in alignment with your values, not someone else's expectations?

Power Pause

Whose rules are you currently living by — family, mentors, industry trends, or your own evolving intuition?

When Your Win Comes from Within

The idea of alignment sounds simple, but it requires courage.

- Courage to say no without guilt
- Courage to choose differently than others
- Courage to build at your pace
- Courage to rest without apology
- Courage to celebrate what matters to you

And what do you do if the finish line keeps moving?

Have you ever thought:

> *"If I can just reach this goal…I'll finally feel successful."*

But when you got there?

➡ *That revenue goal didn't feel high enough*

➡ *That recognition didn't feel like true respect*

➡ *That success still came with exhaustion*

➡ *That milestone still didn't satisfy the longing*

Here's why:

You were running toward the wrong finish line and the bar kept silently being raised. The finish line never stops moving when you're not the one who set it.

I argue that alignment isn't perfection, it's permission. Permission to choose what matters today, delay what can truly wait, and say "No" without defending your decision. Permission to build a life that fits your energy and expand at a pace that honors your humanity.

You aren't eliminating work, you are eliminating the unnecessary. You are removing self-betrayal and beginning to trust yourself. You begin to perform well because you are deciding well.

Instead of becoming the woman the world wants to see, you stop chasing validation. You stop apologizing for boundaries. You stop outsourcing your worth.

At this point success can stop feeling like pressure and can start feeling like belonging in your own life. Instead of a race, success can be a rhythm of quiet confidence.

Power Pause

What decision can I make today that brings me one step closer to the life I actually want?

Even if it is small, especially if it is small.

Alignment Over Achievement

True success starts when what you do matches who you are.

That's alignment — when your calendar, energy, and values all speak the same language.

You stop asking, "Am I doing enough?" and start asking, "Does this feel like me?"

A 2023 Forbes Women survey found that 74 percent of female entrepreneurs who shifted from goal-driven to values-driven planning reported higher satisfaction and lower burnout within a year.

Alignment doesn't mean smaller dreams; it means dreams that fit your life instead of consume it.

There is so much peace in being able to choose who to work with. It's not always possible early in business, but I consider it a measure of my growth.

Do our values align? Are we able to maintain open lines of communication? Do I look forward to our meetings? Those things matter to me.

When I evaluate a prospect, I look for people who are interested in building a relationship — not just chasing a quick win or a discounted service. I also avoid working with clients who don't return calls or emails. If communication breaks down and can't be rebuilt, then either I didn't do something right, or we simply aren't a good fit. When that happens, I refer them to another professional who might serve them better.

Yes, that means if I feel someone isn't a good fit for my business model or values, I will bring in another agent and pass them the business. And sometimes, that same person goes on to have a long and happy relationship with that agent — proof that the right fit matters.

I've heard repeatedly that I can't be everyone's cup of tea, and that I need to find my people. When I gave myself permission to set boundaries around who I work with, I gave myself peace.

Power Pause

Write down your top three core values. Now list one way each shows up — or should show up — in your business, relationships, and daily choices.

The Seasons of Success

Nature doesn't bloom all year. Neither do we.

There are planting seasons — when we build, stretch, and push — and harvest seasons — when we rest, gather, and celebrate. When we expect constant growth, we set ourselves up for disappointment. Recognizing seasons means giving yourself permission to evolve. The goals that fit you five years ago may not fit today — and that's growth, not regression.

As I keep evolving, my family keeps growing, and my business keeps growing my definition of success may change. There are grandchildren to consider now and my parents are aging. Women far outweigh men in the caregiving world and I know I have to plan for changes ahead.

I am planting as much as I can now for a sustainable future. My goal is to continue to find alignment and have the freedom and flexibility to pivot when needed. Longevity comes from balance. I can't burn the candle at both ends and expect to enjoy life happening around me.

We do have struggles in entrepreneurship, absolutely. Times that test us and make us question why we ever embarked on this journey in the first place. Yes, the first years are often more about surviving than thriving.

If you've ever written a business plan you know that they focus on a time frame, generally about 5 years and are broken into annual plans to hit that 5-year mark. The goals in years 1-5 of a business are different than 5-10. Does your plan accurately measure your definition of success? Are you building a business that aligns with your needs?

Build evaluation into your plan and don't be surprised if you fall short in an area. This is not failure, this is a place to adjust, especially in a growth season. When you are hitting a goal or something feels amazing, celebrate it. Immediately.

Power Pause

What season are you in right now — planting, nurturing, or harvesting? What does success look like in this season only, not forever?

The Celebration Gap

We are masters at minimizing wins. We say, "It's not a big deal," "I just got lucky," or "It's nothing, really" and shrug it off like it truly is nothing. This isn't always about trying to be seen as humble, it's also about fear. Fear of not being able to sustain the recognized success.

Fear that we don't deserve it – that voice of failure and self-doubt can really come out in these moments.

Find your courage. Celebration isn't arrogance; it's acknowledgment. It's how we tell our nervous system, "This is safe. I can enjoy this."

A Harvard Business Review study found that teams who practiced "micro-celebrations" — regularly acknowledging small wins — were 31 percent more engaged and resilient during stress cycles.

Did you ever have a manager or team leader ask you to devise your own punishment? The idea that if you don't hit your weekly goal you don't get to do something. I have been asked "what is the thing you aren't going to be able to do if you don't do XYZ?" How do you perform under that stressor? Does it create a positive or negative reaction in you?

I am not ashamed to say that I respond better to positive reinforcement. When the opposite is presented "what are you putting on your calendar to do as a celebration of hitting your weekly goal?" I get excited. I have something to look forward to and work toward. Celebration creates momentum.

As I worked through my process of learning to fail with flying colors, I recognized that even constructive criticism comes across as censure and ridicule. I am unlearning the need to shut down and give up. I have been conditioned to expect failure. If you remember back, even when someone did recognize my work it was still minimized at home. The finish line moved.

The days I do allow myself the celebration still feel a bit strange, but in a good way. It feels decadent and extravagant. How does celebration make you feel? I'll give you a few words I have learned to embrace in celebratory moments: lightness, joy, pride, and confidence.

So light the candle. Share the win. Smile when someone says "Congratulations" and don't explain it away.

Power Pause

List five wins from the past month — big or small. For each, write one sentence that starts with "I'm proud of myself because ..."

Journal Exercise – Define Your Success Statement

Now that you've peeled away old expectations and reconnected to what matters, it's time to define success on your terms.

Identify Your True Metrics

Write three ways you'll measure success this year that have nothing to do with money or numbers. (Examples: peace, progress, presence.)

Create Your Personal Success Statement

Combine them into one sentence:

"Success means living a life that is ______, ______, and ______."

Anchor It in Reality

Post it somewhere visible — planner, phone background, bathroom mirror — and revisit it weekly.

Celebrate Alignment

Each time you make a choice that honors your values over validation, mark it as a win.

 **Power Pause**

How does your new definition of success feel — lighter, clearer, freer? Write it down. Read it aloud. It's yours now.

Closing Reflection – Defining Your Value

Success isn't about arriving at a finish line. It's about creating a rhythm that sustains you.

You've let go of other people's expectations, learned from your failures, and reconnected to yourself. Now, you get to build forward from alignment.

From this point on, success doesn't have to look impressive — it just has to feel true.

Chapter 6: Sustaining Alignment

When the Balance Tips Again

Let's be clear. Living in alignment doesn't mean no pressure, no deadlines, no responsibility. It's about honoring which area needs your attention right now.

You know that moment when everything feels like it's finally running smoothly — the house is in order, your calendar's balanced, and your boundaries are holding firm — and then life shifts?

Suddenly, the stillness you worked so hard to create starts slipping away, and you find yourself back in motion, sprinting toward overwhelm before you even realize it. That's the thing about alignment — it isn't a one-time achievement. It's a rhythm we return to again and again.

It is so easy for me to overcommit. As you learned in the previous chapter I'm a big "Yes" person.

"I can put that on my calendar. I can take on that role. You name it — I can do it!"

The reality is, I can't.

When I put something on my calendar, I have to stick to it. That means saying yes has real consequences. I've gotten into the habit of checking my calendar before I agree to something — because if I don't, I'll be right back in the habit of event-hopping, taking on leadership roles I can't fulfill, and losing family time.

The calendar can feel overwhelming to put into place, but it's the biggest way I protect my time. It's how I ensure that instead of dropping a ball, I am choosing the right one to hold.

I'll give you an example of a recent overcommitment that caused some priorities to shift: this book.

Yep, the one you're reading.

It's something I'd been thinking about doing for a long time. I found Unscrewed Publishing and started writing. But it wasn't on my calendar yet, so other things kept getting prioritized.

Then a group I'm part of — The Girl Cave — offered an event for member authors to promote their books and share their stories. I replied to the email saying I didn't have a published book yet but thought it was a great idea.

Guess who got accepted to the event? Yep — me.

I reached out to Vicky at Unscrewed Publishing and said, "I'm screwed. Unscrew me." And she helped me come up with a plan.

I committed to the event — which also meant committing to writing the book. On a timeline. It's now on my calendar, and I have time blocked for each part of the writing process. Yes, this meant moving some other things and shifting focus for a while to get the book done.

This project has an end date and my alignment will shift again as my priorities shift back. I love the rhythm because when I am choosing wisely, I can't fail.

Power Pause

Think about the last time you said "yes" to something before checking your schedule. What did that choice cost you — time, peace, energy? How might you pause before the next yes?

The Relapse of the Hustle

Even after redefining success, it's easy to fall back into old rhythms. Our culture still rewards visible productivity and constant motion. Rest rarely earns applause.

There will always be a louder voice somewhere telling you how to live, a new standard to measure yourself against, a 'should' you haven't shut down yet. Now you know how to catch it. Because relapse isn't failure — it's feedback.

It's your body whispering, Something's off again.

You might notice it in how you rush through meals, stop journaling, or let guilt creep back in when you slow down. You might notice it in your language — "I just need to get through this week."

Alignment doesn't mean you'll never wobble. It means you recover faster and with more awareness each time. This is no longer life happening at you, no longer productivity for survival, no longer hustle for approval. Your success is no longer defined by outsiders.

Learn the signs you are off course, and bring yourself back to the alignment you are building.

Power Pause

What does "drifting out of alignment" look like in your life — physically, mentally, emotionally? Write three signs you've gone off course.

Building Guardrails – Systems That Support Your Freedom

Alignment thrives when supported by structure. Guardrails don't restrict you; they keep your priorities on track when momentum or chaos threaten to take the wheel.

Think of them as your personal peace-preservers — systems, habits, and boundaries that make it easier to stay true to what matters most.

Time Boundaries: Choose protected blocks each week for deep work, rest, or family — and treat them like client appointments.

Energy Checks: Before saying yes to a new project or event, pause and ask, Does this align with my current goals and energy?

Delegation and Support: Remember — just because you can doesn't mean you should. Hand off, automate, or delay nonessential tasks.

Digital Detox: Schedule tech-free hours each day. Give your nervous system space to breathe.

I've instituted two things into my schedule that have really helped me stay aligned.

Every Monday morning — before I check email or voicemail — I look at my calendar. I review my week and see where I have gaps that need to be filled with client meetings, make sure I'm not overcommitted, and confirm I've blocked admin time to complete follow-ups or paperwork.

The second is that I stop work at 3pm every Friday. I pick my son up from school early (he usually stays until 5:30 for extended care), and we go get ice cream or stop at a park on the way home. It's a small ritual, but it marks the shift from work mode to family mode — and I protect it fiercely.

I also have a standing lunch date with myself. Even if it's only 30 minutes, I disconnect — no laptop, no phone — and I eat, walk, or just breathe. Getting my body moving gets my mind moving, and it improves my mood and creativity.

Knowing your energy patterns is crucial too. For example, that huge drop in energy every day between 2 and 3pm. Pay attention to your body and your rhythms. You'll be amazed at how much more you can accomplish in fewer hours when you're energized and focused instead of forcing productivity from an empty tank.

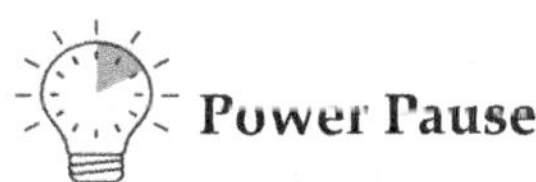

Power Pause

What's one new guardrail you could install this week to protect your time, energy, or mental peace? Commit to testing it for seven days.

The Maintenance Plan

Think of alignment as a living practice, not a static goal. Just like a garden, it needs consistent tending — not perfection, just presence.

Here's a simple framework to stay anchored:

Weekly Check-In: Each Friday, ask yourself — What felt aligned this week? What didn't? Adjust small things before they grow big.

Monthly Reset: Review your calendar and commitments. Are they still serving your goals? Remove or delegate one that doesn't.

Quarterly Reflection: Revisit your "Success Statement" from Chapter 4. Does it still feel true? Update it to match your current season.

Accountability Circle: Connect regularly with people who share your values. Alignment strengthens in community.

Power Pause

What is one rhythm, ritual, or accountability partner that could help you maintain alignment long-term?

Realigning in Real Time

You won't always catch yourself before the drift... and that's okay. Alignment isn't about perfection; it's about responsiveness. When life shifts — a new client, a health scare, a family emergency — your priorities will shift too. Realigning in real time means giving yourself permission to pivot without guilt.

You don't lose your progress when you make an adjustment; you reinforce your wisdom.

Pause. Reassess. Re-enter.

I don't take bad news well. My first reaction to almost anything unexpected is negative. I feel overwhelmed, defensive, even angry. That knee-jerk reaction is something I work on constantly. It's when I most need to pause and reassess.

Past experience always taught me that I was failing — that I couldn't keep up, couldn't reach the bar. When I hear constructive criticism, I still hear it in my Dad's voice from childhood, and I'm immediately transported to that dark, critical space. It doesn't sound or feel constructive at all.

My shift comes when I remember whose bar I'm measuring against. It's in remembering that my success is built from missed opportunities, long nights, and perseverance.

Michael Jordan missed thousands of shots in his career — but he kept shooting. His mindset kept him moving forward. Grit and determination are powerful tools that can move us from failure to success. Find a system that works for you and practice it.

When I get "bad" news now, I get up and walk. I pause before I react. My first response is still negative — but if I can breathe, think, and look for solutions, I usually find that what felt like a closed door is just an alternate path waiting to be explored.

When things get out of alignment, don't stress. You know your way back.

 **Power Pause**

When things feel off, what's your "go-to" reset? A walk, journaling, deep breathing, music, or something else? Make a quick-response list for your future self.

Journal Exercise – Your Alignment Audit

At the end of each month, take fifteen minutes for a simple self-check.

Calendar Check: Does your schedule reflect your stated values?

Energy Check: Are you energized by what you're doing or drained by what you're maintaining?

Connection Check: Who in your circle keeps you grounded — and who consistently pulls you off balance?

Gratitude Check: What moments of alignment felt most fulfilling this month?

Write your answers honestly. No judgment — just data for your next course correction.

Power Pause

What would it look like if you lived from alignment 80 percent of the time — and offered yourself grace for the rest?

Closing Reflection

Alignment isn't about staying perfectly balanced; it's about recognizing the sway and choosing to steady yourself again.

You've redefined success. You've reclaimed your peace. Now you're learning to protect it. This is where transformation becomes lifestyle — where awareness turns into action, and action into freedom.

You aren't trying to prove you deserve this life, you are inhabiting it.

Chapter 7: Becoming the Success You Defined

The Day it Finally Felt Like Success

It wasn't the day I hit a huge goal.

It wasn't the day I outranked someone else in my office.

It was the day I realized I could drink coffee while watching the sunrise…

take a client meeting…

then show up at my son's school for lunch…

and still serve more clients that afternoon.

I was deciding how to spend my time — and that was success.

Success wasn't a finish line – it was a feeling, I was no longer saying I will be successful after I do XYZ, or when everything is perfect. I realized the win is already happening because success isn't measured in checklists, but rather by how fully I belong in my story.

That is alignment.

Look at your life and answer:

> *What is one moment recently where you thought "I love that I get to do this?"*
>
> *What part of your day feels like the reward for all your hard work?*

Write it down, that's success.

You Didn't Change — You Came Home to Yourself

This journey wasn't about becoming someone new. It was about removing everything that told you that you weren't enough as you were.

By questioning the expectations, challenging the comparison traps, and releasing guilt as a default setting, you broke up with hustle as a personality trait and replaced striving with alignment.

That is a transformation most people never experience.

You didn't upgrade your life – you upgraded your power.

Power sounds like:

> *"I trust myself."*
>
> *"I like who I am in this life."*
>
> *"My pace is the right pace."*
>
> *"This success is mine."*

Journal Exercise

What is something you once apologized for that you now proudly claim?

Examples:

Your ambition

Your boundaries

Your rest

Your joy

Your confidence

Write it. Read it back. Own it.

When You Stop Asking for Approval

For so long, success required a witness. This is what research tells us:

When you finally believe you're enough before anyone else approves you, everything changes. It's no longer about passing tests, getting likes, checking boxes, or earning someone else's nod. According to a 2023 narrative review, the ability to extend compassion to yourself depends on whether you feel worthy. (Muris et al., 2023)

And here's the kicker: value for many women has been built on external approvals — performance, appearance, praise, "being liked." Research shows when your self-worth depends on those external things, you become vulnerable to feeling like a failure every time life shifts. (Crocker, 2011)

But what if the story changed? What if success started with internal approval—"I approve of me, whether this attempt works or not"—and failure stopped being a judgment and became a tool? That shift isn't just linguistic; it's physiological. You stop bracing for the verdict, and you start moving with purpose. You stop subsisting on applause, and you start operating from truth.

When you tell yourself: I am enough right now, you stop chasing rescue. You stop needing permission. You stop fearing the drop. Because you've anchored your worth beneath the outcome. That is where real power begins.

Now that you don't need a stamp of approval, your decisions no longer sound like:

"Do you think I'm doing okay?"

"Is this the right path?"

"Will others think this is enough?"

Now your decisions sound like:

"This is what alignment looks like for me."

"This is how I choose to show up today."

"I don't need you to understand my success."

You are no longer waiting for a gold star to feel proud. You are bold, beautiful, successful, and enough al on your own.

Which of these statements feels like your next bold step?

I don't need permission to protect my time

I don't need applause to celebrate myself

I don't need validation to know I'm doing enough

I don't need to match anyone else's pace

Choose one → speak it out loud.

Let your voice hear your power.

When Success Stops Being Performance

When you no longer show up to prove you're good enough, you start to show up because:

The work matters

The people matter

You matter

Even your ambition is different now. It's not fueled by fear of falling behind — it's fueled by joy, service, purpose, freedom, and pride. You're not chasing a life you hope will impress other people. You're building a life that deeply satisfies you.

Setting boundaries hasn't always been well-received for me, but it truly is a hallmark of my success. I'll pick on my husband here. In the beginning of my entrepreneurial journey, he wasn't my biggest cheerleader. I could have given in and stopped, but I didn't. I chose myself because I can see what he can't – the finish line I have set for myself.

For him, tangibles are easier to believe in. It's extremely hard for him to take chances and put full faith in an idea that may not come to fruition. And that's ok. He is wonderful at providing and making sure we have what we need while I chase my dream. At one point he surprised me with a new laptop even when I knew he wasn't fully on board yet.

The truth is that in the beginning I wanted his approval. I needed him to be my cheerleader. And my performance suffered when he wasn't. I felt failure keenly in the beginning. The day I said to myself it doesn't matter what he thinks now, it matters what I think and feel, it matters that I succeed because I believe in this, I started a new journey.

He has come to some of my events and has met a couple of my clients. There is a shift happening as he starts to see what I have been working toward come closer to what I have told him is possible.

The day I released my need for his approval I released the expectation of failure. I gave myself permission to strive for my version of success.

Confidence Doesn't Need Volume

Your confidence isn't loud. It doesn't need to be. The kind of confidence that transforms isn't about decibels. It's built quietly, steadily, every day. It's built by knowing you have been through enough to trust yourself to see what matters and choose your path. It's built by not abandoning yourself any more.

When you finally believe you're enough before anyone else approves you, everything changes. External approval stops being the driving force. You're no longer performing for someone else's verdict — you're showing up because you're aligned with your own truth.

Research supports this: A study of women in leadership development programs found that when women experienced a shift in their internal confidence — not just their technical skill — they were far more likely to act with clarity, presence and authority. (Herbst, Roux & Naidoo, 2024)

In another review of confidence and leadership, researchers noted that when women depend on external approval for their self-worth (appearance, others' praise, performance), their confidence becomes fragile — susceptible to any change of outcome. (Crocker, 2011)

This is why your steady kind of confidence matters more than the loud kind. You walk into rooms like you belong because you do. You carry yourself differently because your internal compass is calibrated.

Do you remember walking into a room as a child and instantly meeting a new best friend? That's the feeling you get when you simply belong as yourself. It doesn't matter the room you walked into, you know you belong there.

The first time this happened for me in business I walked into a Marshall County Chamber after hours meeting – it was Mardi Gras themed and I networked my way into finding a new home for Arnold, my goat. Since that night, I have joined the chamber, made amazing new connections, and gained some clients. I am happy, confident, and fulfilled. My sense of belonging has built a sense of community for me there and I look for ways to give back.

The Girl Cave gives a sense of belonging also. The women welcome you… literally with open arms. It doesn't matter who you are or where you come from, you belong in that room and you have found a tribe that will support and uplift you.

Confidence doesn't need volume. It needs truth, clarity, ownership, presence.

Walk into every room like you belong – because you do.

Journal Exercise

What is something you do now, with confidence, that used to terrify you?

What changed in you to make that possible?

The New Normal: You Are Winning While Living Well

I remember it clearly — fumbling to turn off the alarm clock at 4am, stumbling to the coffee pot, and settling in to work on my laptop hoping I hadn't woken my family up. I told myself this is success: early mornings, late nights, endless lists.

Anxious cold sweats counted as progress. Exhaustion counted as proof.

Those days? They're gone. The new normal is:

> *Achievement without self-abandonment — you closed the deal and still held space for your joy.*
>
> *Ambition without apology — you raised your fee and didn't whisper an excuse.*
>
> *Progress without panic — you moved forward and let your nervous system rest.*
>
> *Confidence without comparison — you measured your win by how you felt, not by someone else's scoreboard.*

I want you to revel in aligned success. Wake up each day anticipating good things. Gone is that old sense of dread. I want you to feel so whole and so proud that you forget what it was like to feel stretched thin. Change your narrative so that the smile you show the world isn't staged — it's real.

You are no longer fighting for success. You are thriving inside it.

Research backs that when women anchor their worth inside—rather than seeking others' approval—they experience greater resilience, less anxiety about performance, and a deeper sense of belonging. (Mandal, 2023)

Power Pause - Anchor the Win

Write 3 things you have now that earlier-you used to wish for. Circle the one that feels like the biggest "I made it."

Sit with that pride for a full minute. Yes — set a timer and let it land. ⏱

You Become the Example

Women around you see the shift.

They feel the difference.

They start asking:

> *"How did you do it?"*
>
> *"What changed?"*
>
> *"How can I get there too?"*

I'll never forget the day it happened. I was chatting with a friend — someone who knows me almost too well. She'd heard some of my internal battles, seen the catalog of my failures, watched me stumble and rise again. And she looked me in the eyes and said:

"I think you are just so inspiring."

My first thought: What? Me?

Because if anything, I felt inspired by her. She knows I'm not perfect. She knows I still have off days. What I realized was that she saw all of that and was still proud of me. Her admiration wasn't because everything was going perfectly for me. It was rooted in the fact that I kept showing up — every day, for myself, for my business, for my friends and family. Once I let go of being uncomfortable with my story, I started seeing the signs of success not only in what I did, but in who I was becoming.

And that's when I knew: I am no longer just living my story. I am leading with it.

I am proof that there's a better way than burnout.

I am someone's permission slip to choose peace over performance.

I am redefining what success looks like — in real time.

When you allow your journey to be visible, you become the hope someone else needed.

You become the path for them.

Closing Reflection — You Are the Win

I remember what it felt like to chase the next milestone — the swoosh of a badge earned, the relief of a meeting finally booked, the sense of breathing when a deadline was met. I didn't realize: I had been treating success like a destination. As if life would begin once I crossed the finish line. Now I know: success isn't a finish line.

Success comes with every morning you choose your values instead of someone else's definition, every boundary you hold that protects the peace you've earned, and every celebration you allow honoring the woman you fought so hard to become.

This is your life. Your power. Your win. Your success. Own it.

And here's what comes next: you're stepping into a new chapter where joy is part of the definition—not just the result. In Chapter 8, we'll bring celebration to the front row, not the backseat. Because you've lived long enough to know: when you win while living well, you rewrite the culture not just for yourself—but for every woman watching.

You've Been Winning for Years

You've been winning for years. You just haven't been *counting* your wins.

I used to walk through my days keeping score in my head — clients landed, launches launched, hours logged. Yet each night I'd close my laptop with the same whisper: Was that enough?

Women are trained to act like success is no big deal. We downplay accomplishments, focus on what's unfinished, and measure where we fall short. Even worse, when we do achieve a goal we move that goal post immediately, reinforcing that it's never enough.

We brush off victories with:

> *"It's nothing."*
>
> *"It's small."*
>
> *"It's not as impressive as hers."*
>
> *"I'll celebrate when..."*

Don't hold on to your wins like a secret. Those wins are your story, and your story deserves to be told. Today, we rewrite the rule: Every win counts. Small wins especially count. Small wins stack. Small wins build momentum. Small wins make big success possible.

When we intentionally acknowledge even the small wins, our brain activates its reward-system, releasing dopamine and reinforcing behavior. Also, failing to celebrate contributes to burnout — skipping the pause means skipping the signal our body and mind need.

 **Power Pause - Spot the Win**

Think back on the last 48 hours:

Something you completed

Something you handled with grace

Something that didn't break you this time

Something you chose differently

Write one win here:

"I'm proud that I ____*."*

Say it out loud. Seriously. Let your ears hear it.

Why Celebration Changes Everything

I'll admit it — I've walked past victories as if they were already old news. I'd land a client. I'd finish a project. I'd hit the number. But instead of pausing, I'd glance at the next check-box and sprint on. One afternoon, my shoulders still humming from the win, I heard a whisper in my body: You didn't let yourself feel it. Because I didn't.

When we intentionally acknowledge even the small wins, our brain activates its reward-system, releasing dopamine and reinforcing behavior. Also, failing to celebrate contributes to burnout — skipping the pause means skipping the signal our body and mind need.

Celebration does three powerful things:

It reinforces the good choice — *your brain remembers and wants to repeat it.*

It builds identity — *you look in the mirror and say, "I'm someone who succeeds."*

It boosts confidence — *momentum kicks in, motivation deepens, joy grows.*

But let's be clear: celebration is not indulgence.

Celebration is a strategy.

When you acknowledge progress, you accelerate it.

When you ignore progress, you sabotage it.

This is why perfectionists burn out: they only celebrate the flawless finish and ignore every step it took to get there.

One of the biggest wins I celebrate is being able to interact with my son at home Without A Phone In My Hand. I am not checking email, scrolling facebook, nor looking for the next text message. There were many years when work consumed me and I couldn't unplug. How do I teach my son balance and connection if I myself am not balanced and connected?

Being able to be connected without worry, feels free. I'm also proud of what I am able to share with my son in those moments.

Celebration Isn't a Reward — It's a Requirement

I remember sitting at my desk at the end of a 12hr day and feeling nothing. Am I doing all of this for numbness? What am I sacrificing for if I can't feel joy? I told myself the real celebration would come "when the big number hit" or "once the launch was complete."

What I didn't realise then was: you don't have to wait until you:

⊘ *hit the revenue milestone*

⊘ *fit the jeans*

⊘ *finish the project*

⊘ *earn the title*

to feel proud. You can celebrate:

✨ *starting*

✨ *trying*

✨ *learning*

✨ *finishing*

✨ *surviving*

✨ *pivoting*

✨ *resting*

✨ *choosing joy*

✨ *coming back tomorrow*

✨ *not giving up*

Because you deserve celebration because you keep going and endurance is sacred.

How do we create endurance? It's not from motivation, let's be real, you aren't always going to feel motivated in your life or your business. Endurance is created in good habits – and celebrating your wins needs to be one of those habits. The positive reinforcement. The good feelings, those can help you keep going through adversity. You have the freedom to choose the wins and how you celebrate them.

In the next section, we'll lean into how this rhythm of celebration frees you from needing everything to be perfect—and honors the motion of progress instead.

You're Allowed to Feel Good on Purpose

There was a time when joy felt dangerous. Because if you celebrated too soon, you feared:

dropping the ball

losing your edge

being judged

inviting disappointment

So you kept joy at arm's length, until everything was perfect. Until you had "earned" it. Until it felt safe. Joy is fuel — not a finish line. Joy gives you the energy to keep going. You have survived enough hard; you don't have to earn your sunshine. Now it is time to feel good on purpose. We are going to honor progress over perfection.

Power Pause

Circle the one that feels hardest to believe:

I deserve to celebrate my progress

Rest counts as a win

I am allowed to enjoy the life I'm building

Pride is not selfish

Joy does not require permission

That belief is your next breakthrough.

Progress Over Perfection

Perfection says: "If it isn't flawless, it doesn't count."

Alignment says: "You showed up — and that counts."

Success isn't built on perfection. It's built on trial and error, courage, repetition, and bouncing back.

Know that every step forward is a win, every lesson learned is a win, and every pivot is a win. Progress is proof of success in motion.

Let me tell you, there are days I show up messy. The important thing is I show up. Sometimes we leave the house late or have to bring a child on an appointment.

Not every client is going to say "Yes" to a plan you have shown them. Celebrate the fact that you overcame adversity to show up. Learn something from the client that said "No" – was it something in your control or not? If it's in your control do better; if it isn't, let it go.

If you are moving your life or business in the right direction, I want you to celebrate. Regardless of the end result, you showed up, showed out, and gave it your all to move the needle forward.

You are a rock star! Celebrate yourself.

When You Celebrate, Others Join You

Here's the amazing ripple effect:

When you celebrate yourself…

- ✨ *Other women feel safer celebrating too*
- ✨ *Your kids learn confidence by watching you*
- ✨ *Your success becomes a normal part of life — not a surprise*
- ✨ *Joy becomes contagious*

You give permission for others to shine without shrinking themselves.

You become the example that women can succeed and feel good doing it.

That is leadership. That is legacy.

Power Pause

Who in your life needs to see you celebrate more?

Your children? Partner? Clients? Employees? Yourself?

How will you show them joy this week?

Journal Exercise - Build a Life Where Wins Don't Go Unnoticed

Celebration shouldn't be rare. It should be a rhythm.

Here are 4 simple celebration structures you can integrate right away:

1: Daily "I Did That" List: Not a to-do list, a done list. Tonight, write:

Three things you completed

One thing you're proud of

One thing you're grateful for

Repeat tomorrow. That's momentum.

2: Weekly Win Ritual: Review your week:

What worked this week?

What did I learn?

What deserves applause?

Then actually celebrate it because your nervous system loves closure.

3: Monthly Milestone Check-In

Grab your Success Definition from Chapter 4:

✔ *Am I living aligned with my values?*

✔ *Does this month feel like success?*

✔ *What small win deserves a spotlight?*

Dopamine reset = motivation reset.

4: "High-Five Future Me" Notes

Write a letter each month from your future self and seal it. Remind yourself that: You kept going, you chose peace, you are built a life you love.

Open it next month and write a new one. Repeat.

Joy documented becomes joy amplified.

Power Pause — Celebrate THIS

Write 3 wins you've achieved while reading this book:

1. ________________________________
2. ________________________________
3. ________________________________

Now say: "I did that. And I'm proud." Really say it. Let pride be allowed.

Closing Reflection — Celebration as Your Success Language

From this moment forward track progress, honor effect, celebrate growth, and count every win.

Because…

You are not a woman who waits for permission anymore.

You are not a woman who downplays her power.

You are not a woman who hides her joy.

You are a woman who celebrates the life she's worked for.

Every win.

Every milestone.

Every moment that feels like freedom.

This joy is yours.

Next, let's take back the pen. Write your own rules.

Chapter 9: Failing With Flying Colors: Your Turn

You Didn't Come This Far to Stay the Same

You came here to:

> *rewrite your rules*
>
> *heal your relationship with success*
>
> *and build a life that actually feels like yours.*

And now? It's time to take everything you've learned and put it into motion. This chapter is where the shift becomes action, where the story you tell about yourself moves from past-tense to possibility, where failure no longer means "the end" but becomes the evidence of growth.

Where you step into the identity of a woman who says: "If I fall — I rise with more data, more strength, more clarity."

That is failing with flying colors. That is unstoppable.

Power Pause

Take a moment right now and breathe. Deeply. Intentionally. Say this:

"I am not behind. I am becoming."

What You've Outgrown

Let's put it all on the page — clearly and unapologetically.

What beliefs are no longer welcome in this chapter of your life?

I must do everything perfectly

I must earn rest

I must meet others' expectations to feel worthy

I must hide my ambition

I must say yes to everything

I must apologize for my success

I must choose between family and business

I must compare myself to others

I must pretend I'm fine

I must always be strong

Which ones are gone for good? Cross. Them. Out.

If there are some not listed - write them down then Cross. Them. Out.

Journal Exercise

Write a short goodbye letter to the old expectations.

Something like: "Thank you for getting me this far. But I don't need you to lead anymore."

Release it, you are stepping into something bigger.

What You're Running Toward Now

Your new chapter is not "less stress."

Your new chapter is more of the things you've always wanted. More joy, more presence, more purpose, more alignment, and more celebration! Success from the inside out means that:

> *You're not chasing — you're choosing.*
>
> *You're not performing — you're embodying.*
>
> *You're not reacting — you're designing.*

This is where the magic starts.

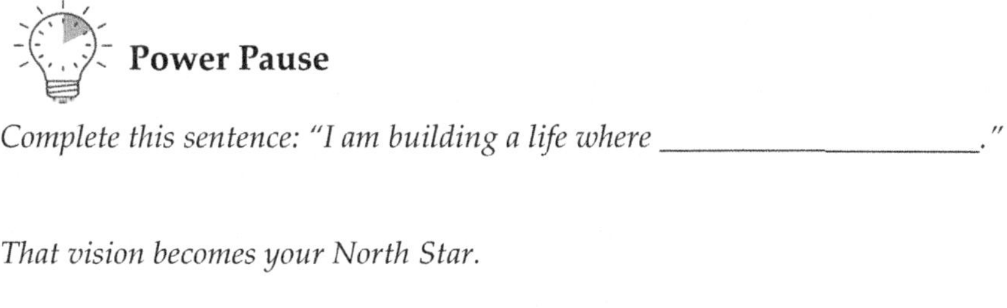

Power Pause

Complete this sentence: "I am building a life where ____________________."

That vision becomes your North Star.

Step 1 — Your Success Statement

You already unlocked the truth: Success isn't a destination — it's a definition. Now you capture it in one powerful statement.

Use this formula:

> *Success = (What I value most) + (How I want to feel while achieving it) + (The freedom I commit to protecting)*

Example:

> *"Success = meaningful impact + joyful, calm confidence + flexibility to show up for my family."*

Now it's your turn:

Write your success statement:

____

____

____

This becomes your compass.

 **Power Pause**

Say your success statement out loud. Let your nervous system feel what's possible.

Step 2 — Define 3 Goals That Align

We are not setting hustle goals anymore. We are setting alignment goals.

Choose one for each Core Area:

♥ *Self*

🏡 *Family & Relationships*

💼 *Business & Purpose*

Ask:

Does this goal match my success statement?

Does pursuing it make my life better today?

Will this feel like a win even before it's complete?

Write them in:

♥ *Self Goal:* ________________________________

🏡 *Family Goal:* ________________________________

💼 *Business Goal:* ____________________________

Step 3 — Failure-Proof Your Path

YES — we expect obstacles. YES — we embrace the pivots.

Create your Failing With Flying Colors Strategy:

✅ *What will I do when I feel overwhelmed?*

✓ *What will I do when progress slows?*

✓ *How will I speak to myself when doubt appears?*

✓ *Who can I lean on for support?*

Write it:

"When I hit a challenge, I will ______________________________ __________."

We didn't say "if I hit a challenge". We know we WILL hit challenges. Challenge doesn't mean "stop," it means "strategize, then continue."

Setbacks teach us something essential.

They are the feedback that give us a chance to pivot, the drive to push in a new direction. I work in a commission industry and not every sale sticks. If I get a reversal and my goal line moves back it can get discouraging. I used to wallow in that negative and start to panic about what to do next.

Now I know my metrics. I know how many calls I need to make, how many appointments I need to run to get a new sale on the books. My conversion ratio maps out for me the steps I need to take. Often the next person that I educate and converts to a client moves me further ahead than I was.

This reinforces that failing with flying colors is your lived reality — not a theory.

Step 4 — Celebration on Schedule

Success must feel good, not just look good.

Choose your monthly milestone ritual:

Family celebration

Solo treat day

Spa night

Adventure outing

A day off

New outfit

A nap and zero guilt

Something else: __________

Put it in your calendar because this is non-negotiable.

Power Pause

Write this where you'll see it often: "I succeed out loud now."

Every step is worthy of applause. Especially the messy ones.

Your Next Chapter Begins With a Vision

You are leaving behind the "not enough" era and stepping into the I am becoming era. To anchor that truth, we close this chapter with a guided visualization — your monthly ritual for aligned momentum.

Future Self Visualization Ritual

Find a quiet place. Breathe in deeply for 4 seconds…hold for 2…exhale for 6…

Now imagine yourself 12 months from now. You wake up in the life you designed, not the life you were handed. Not the life you were pressured into, but the life you built — on purpose.

Picture your future self's morning…

> *How does she start her day?*
>
> *How does she carry herself?*
>
> *How does she choose her schedule?*
>
> *How does she speak to herself?*
>
> *How does she feel in her relationships?*
>
> *What is she celebrating this month?*

Observe the way she looks at you — with gratitude. You are the one who did the work, allowed the rest, took the risks, released the guilt, and kept showing up. You are her beginning and she is your proof that failing with flying colors was worth it.

Power Pause — Bring Her Closer

Answer these 3 prompts:

1. *In one word, how does she feel?* ______________________________
2. *What is one habit she practices every week?* _____________________

3. *What is one boundary she holds without apology?* ______________

Those are your action priorities for the next 30 days. Because every aligned decision you make brings you closer to her.

I walk out of my house each morning with the same schedule, the same demands, the same un-spoken pressure that I've always carried. But today—something is different. My steps are lighter. My calendar still buzzes, but my mind feels more still. I have been working on failing with flying colors: reframing success, healing shame, reclaiming my time, defining my values, stepping into confidence.

Conclusion — You Are the Success Story

You started this book because something inside you whispered: "There has to be a better way." And you listened. Look at the journey you've taken:

✅ *Chapter 1 — You recognized the invisible pressure*

✅ *Chapter 2 — You redefined failure as growth*

✅ *Chapter 3 — You reclaimed your identity beyond hustle*

✅ *Chapter 4 — You rejected guilt as a measure of worth*

✅ *Chapter 5 — You rebuilt success on your terms*

✅ *Chapter 6 — You learned to sustain alignment*

✅ *Chapter 7 — You became the success you defined*

✅ *Chapter 8 — You celebrated the wins you used to hide*

✅ *Chapter 9 — You designed the next chapter of your life*

This is transformation: Not loud. Not flashy. Not performative.

But deeply rooted. Steady. Intentional. Yours.

The World Needs Women Who Choose Themselves

Because when a woman decides:

"I am enough — and I get to define what success looks like," everything around her expands:

- *Her family sees possibility*
- *Her community feels hope*
- *Her children learn confidence*
- *Other women rise, too*

You have become the example you once needed.

Your Story Continues With Courage

Right now, you may feel:

Excited

Proud

Nervous

Strong

Tender

Determined

All of that is welcome. Every sunrise is a reminder that you get another chance to make another decision and reach another win. Each aligned choice you make from this moment forward strengthens your success, protects your peace, honors your joy, and builds your legacy.

You do not have to sprint to stay worthy. You do not have to hustle to stay successful. You only have to keep choosing the woman you've become.

A Final Power Pause — Speak This Truth

Hand on heart.

Deep breath in.

Say this slowly:

> *"I am already living a successful life.*
>
> *And I am only getting stronger."*

One more time:

> *"I am already enough.*
>
> *I am allowed to enjoy what I've built."*

Let that truth settle in your bones.

An Invitation

Now go forward and live loudly, rest deeply, celebrate boldly, choose joy relentlessly, rise unapologetically, and define success every single day

And when you fail — as every brave woman does? Fail with flying colors.

Because every chapter of your becoming is a victory.

This is not the end. This is your beginning.

Acknowledgments

I wrote this book because no woman should have to chase someone else's definition of success — or feel like she's failing while doing it. And I certainly couldn't have written it without the amazing (and occasionally insane) village that carried me through.

First, to my husband — thank you for always being there. After more than a decade together, you know we speak completely different languages, but you show up for our family in a million ways I see sometimes only after the chaos quiets down. I appreciate them all.

To my son — thanks for morning cuddles, post-school car-pool talks, and for reminding me every day what this redefined success is really for.

To my parents — I quite literally would not be here without you. So yeah… maybe you should've been listed first.

To my sister — having to grow up with me in the same house deserves some kind of medal. Love you … and those wild little nephews of mine.

To my friends, near and far — I'm so glad I don't wander this earth alone. Special shoutout to Angela and Kandice, who've patiently endured my long rants and my overthinking brain. You make the messy stuff feel less lonely.

To Holly — thank you for giving me my start in financial services, for putting up with my chaos, and for dragging me on those unforgettable animal-rescue missions. Your faith that I could get my act together helped make the woman I'm becoming possible.

To the women of Women Mean Business Platform — thank you for sharing your raw stories, your wins, heartbreaks, hopes, and for trusting me with them. You are living proof that success can look many ways, and I'm honored to build this community with you.

To Vicky at Unscrewed Publishing — thanks for sorting through my messy drafts, helping me find my voice, and turning chaos into chapters. Your patience, honesty, and guidance turned ideas into a book.

To every woman who ever whispered, "I'm not enough" — this book is for you. I want you to see (as I see) that you already are.

Finally, to all the quiet moments, the messy days, the tears, and the triumphs — this book is for what you've taught me. Because you mattered. And I remembered.

P.S. If you helped me at any point — even with a smile, a cup of coffee, or a shoulder to lean on — consider yourself thanked. I couldn't have done this without the everyday heroes reading this now.

Made in the USA
Coppell, TX
20 January 2026

66374494R00075